astro city
private lives

kurt busiek
writer

brent eric anderson
artist

alex ross
cover art

graham nolan
artist,
"the deep dark woods"

alex sinclair &
wendy broome
colors

comicraft's john roshell
& jimmy betancourt
lettering & design

astro city created by **busiek, anderson & ross**

VERTIGO

RICHARD STARKINGS
Art Director

Kristy Quinn	Editor — Original Series and Collected Edition
Jessica Chen	Assistant Editor — Original Series
Jeb Woodard	Group Editor — Collected Editions
Robbin Brosterman	Design Director — Books
Shelly Bond	VP & Executive Editor — Vertigo
Diane Nelson	President
Dan DiDio and Jim Lee	Co-Publishers
Geoff Johns	Chief Creative Officer
Amit Desai	Senior VP — Marketing & Global Franchise Management
Nairi Gardiner	Senior VP — Finance
Sam Ades	VP — Digital Marketing
Bobbie Chase	VP — Talent Development
Mark Chiarello	Senior VP — Art, Design & Collected Editions
John Cunningham	VP — Content Strategy
Anne DePies	VP — Strategy Planning & Reporting
Don Falletti	VP — Manufacturing Operations
Lawrence Ganem	VP — Editorial Administration & Talent Relations
Alison Gill	Senior VP — Manufacturing & Operations
Hank Kanalz	Senior VP — Editorial Strategy & Administration
Jay Kogan	VP — Legal Affairs
Derek Maddalena	Senior VP — Sales & Business Development
Dan Miron	VP — Sales Planning & Trade Development
Nick Napolitano	VP — Manufacturing Administration
Carol Roeder	VP — Marketing
Eddie Scannell	VP — Mass Account & Digital Sales
Susan Sheppard	VP — Business Affairs
Courtney Simmons	Senior VP — Publicity & Communications
Jim (Ski) Sokolowski	VP — Comic Book Specialty & Newsstand Sales

Special thanks to: Ellie Collins, Robbie Geiss, Sandy Oh & Dottie Thomas

Library of Congress
Cataloging-in-Publication Data

Busiek, Kurt, author.
Astro City : Private Lives / Kurt Busiek, writer ; Brent Anderson, artist.
pages cm
Summary: "When you're the Silver Adept, one of Astro City's newest and most powerful mystic heroes, your life is full of magic, battle, demons, apocalypses and more. When you're the Adept's personal assistant, though, life gets really weird. A look at the woman behind the hero. Collects ASTRO CITY #11–16"— Provided by publisher.
ISBN 978-1-4012-5824-5
1. Graphic novels. I. Anderson, Brent Eric, illustrator. II. Title.

PN6728.A79B79 2015
741.5'973--dc23
2014046034

ASTRO CITY: PRIVATE LIVES

Published by DC Comics. Compilation Copyright © 2015 Juke Box Productions. All Rights Reserved.

Originally published in single magazine form as ASTRO CITY 11–16 © 2014 Juke Box Productions. Astro City, its logos, symbols, prominent characters featured in this volume and the distinctive likeness thereof are trademarks of Juke Box Productions. VERTIGO is a trademark of DC Comics. The stories, characters and incidents featured in this publication are entirely fictional. DC Comics does not read or accept unsolicited submissions of ideas, stories or artwork.

DC Comics, 4000 Warner Blvd., Burbank, CA 91522
A Warner Bros. Entertainment Company.
Printed by RR Donnelley, Salem, VA, USA. 9/4/15. First Printing.

ISBN: 978-1-4012-5824-5

c⊗ntents

There is a house, in Astro City.

If you saw it, all you'd see is a Victorian brownstone on a tiny cul de sac tucked in among the streets south of Government Hill.

Converted from a single-family home to apartments sometime in the 1950s, then converted back in the 1980s.

When I look at it, though...

...I SEE SOMETHING ELSE.

HEY, GREV. HOW WAS THE NIGHT?

QUIET, FOR A CHANGE. NOT MUCH TO DO. SHE'S NOT *UP* YET, THOUGH.

SHE'S NOT *UP?*

BUT THEN, I WORK HERE. THE HOUSE DOESN'T *HIDE* ITSELF FROM ME.

...THE SILVER ADEPT, CHAMPION OF THE LIGHT. RENOWNED ACROSS COUNTLESS REALITIES. THE SAVIOR OF MORE LIVING SOULS THAN YOU CAN POSSIBLY IMAGINE.

AND YADDITA YADDITA YADDITA...

BOSS!

NNNNNAAAH... GO 'WAY...TOO EARLY...

I WISH I COULD SAY I DIDN'T SEE HER LIKE THIS OFTEN. BUT TO TELL THE TRUTH, IT'S RARE FOR HER TO BE UP AND READY TO GO WHEN I ARRIVE.

STILL...

IT'S 8:52.

I SET THE ALARM. I SWEAR I SET THE ALARM...

I DON'T DOUBT IT.

WE GO THROUGH MORE CLOCKS.

I WAS IN ONE OF THE ENFOLDED DIMENSIONS. I CALMED AN IFRIT. THERE WAS A CELEBRATION, IT WENT LATE.

BUT THERE WAS SUSHI. AMAZING, FANTASTIC SUSHI.

AT LEAST, I THINK IT WAS SUSHI...

LORD COLQUHOUN?!

I'M IN A JAM, LASS! NEED HER HELP!

AH...SHE'S REALLY *SOCKED IN*, SIR. IT LOOKS *URGENT*, BUT IF I CAN ASK -- *HOW* URGENT?

THE *BORDERS* OF THE RIFT... THEY WON'T FULLY COLLAPSE FOR *THREE DAYS*. SO I SUPPOSE THERE'S *THAT* LONG, IN TERMS OF HUMAN SURVIVAL ON EARTH.

BUT, LASS, MY *ANCESTRAL ESTATE* -- IT WON'T SURVIVE 'TIL DAWN, AT THIS RATE.

I *SEE.* ANY *OTHER* WEEK, I'M SURE SHE'D BE *RIGHT THERE.* IT'S JUST A REALLY BAD -- WAIT. DO YOU STILL HAVE THE *ORB OF EBON STILLNESS?*

I WAS CATALOGUING THE *UPPER-MEDIUM ORDER OF ARTIFACTS* LAST WEEK, AND --

YES, YES! BUT -- ARE YOU SUGGESTING I PURCHASE HER HELP?

NOT *EXACTLY.*

HOLD ON, I'LL GET RIGHT *BACK* TO YOU.

PING CHANGE OF *PLANS*, BOSS.

YOU'RE NOT TAKING THE *BLACK PATHS.* IT'LL BE A STRAIGHT SHOT THROUGH THE WILLOWAYS. YOU'RE GOING TO *STRATHCLYDE.*

WHAT? BUT --

I EXPLAIN COLQUHOUN'S *PROBLEM*, AND...

BUT I NEED *MORE* TIME, NOT LESS. I MEAN, I DON'T DOUBT OLD LORD AL'S IN A *REAL FIGHT*, BUT --

HE'S GOT THE *ORB*, KIM. THERE'S *THREE DAYS' WORK* TO DO ON THOSE TEXTS, AND WE CAN'T *CLEAR* THREE DAYS.

BUT HE'S GOT A *NULL DIMENSION.* TIME MOVES AT A *CRAWL* IN THE ORB. SO YOU CAN --

BRILLIANT. YOU'RE *BRILLIANT.*

I BEAT BACK WHATEVER *ELDRITCH HORROR* HE WAS TRYING TO CHAT UP, POP INTO THE ORB, SPEND ALL THE TIME I *NEED*...

...AND I'M BACK IN A MATTER OF *HOURS.*

SEND HIM THE *TEXTS*, AND I'LL PICK THEM UP THERE.

ONLY TROUBLE IS, YOU'LL BE *OUT OF TOUCH* THE REST OF THE DAY. THE AETHERNET CAN'T HANDLE THE *TIME DISTORTION.*

PUSH EMERGENCIES ON *GRIMOIRE,* THE *HANGED MAN*...

...EVEN THE *COLLEGIUM,* IF NECESSARY. ANYTHING ELSE *PRESSING?*

I'VE GOT *MODI* AND MAGNI STILL TO BUMP, AND A *PAROLE CONSULT* ON MR. MALEFIC. BUT THAT SHOULDN'T BE A PROBLEM.

PERFECT! LET'S *DO* IT!

AND FINALLY, THERE WAS A LITTLE *FREE TIME.* A LATE LUNCH, SOME WORK AT THE WHEEL --

..YOU COME BY AT, SAY, *SEVEN-THIRTY,* I SHOULD BE DONE. AWESOME, BEL. SEE YOU *THEN.*

YOU SEEM LIKE YOU'RE *SETTLING IN* WELL.

AM I?

I GUESS I *AM.* THERE'S A GREAT *ARTS COMMUNITY* HERE IN ASTRO CITY. MUSIC, READINGS, GALLERIES. WE WERE *ISOLATED,* OUTSIDE VICTORIA.

YEAH, I'M *ADJUSTING,* ALL RIGHT. AND *YOU?*

NOT MUCH OF A *CHANGE,* NOT FOR ME.

BUT HERE, IT'S *DIFFERENT.* I'M MEETING PEOPLE, *GETTING* SOMEWHERE WITH MY CERAMICS...

I STAY MOSTLY TO THE *FIELDS,* AND AM CONTENT TO DO SO. BUT MY SONS LOVE THE *BOOKS* YOU BRING THEM.

THEY ALREADY SPEAK OF *TRAVEL,* OF --

WHAT IN...?

MAY YOUR DEATH BE *SWIFT* AND YOUR OFFSPRING *HUNGRY,* WOMAN.

YOU ARE NOT THE *SILVER ADEPT.* TELL HER THE *NIGHTFLYING LORD* IS HERE, WITH *THE QUEEN OF DUST AND DECAY* AND *TUMORR.*

BRING HER *FORTH.*

SHE'S... NOT *AVAILABLE* AT PRESENT. IF I COULD TAKE A *MESSAGE...?*

NOT PRESENT?

AUDIENCE ARRANGED, MEAT-FEMALE! NOT KNOW *IMPORT?* NOT KNOW HOW BRIEF PEACE BETWEEN CLANS?

IF LIED TO...

NO, NO -- WAIT, CALM DOWN. NO ONE SAID ANYTHING ABOUT BEING *LIED* TO. THE ADEPT WAS UNEXPECTEDLY *CALLED AWAY* ON URGENT BUSINESS.

BUT TELL ME WHAT'S *GOING ON,* AND --

THE *AR-MANG* HAS BEEN BORN. BUT HE -- OR SHE -- CANNOT BE *FOUND.*

IF THE AR-MANG IS *NOT FOUND,* THERE WILL BE TURMOIL AMONG THE CLANS OF THE STONE SEA. TURMOIL AND *DEATH.*

THE ADEPT PROMISED A SOLUTION. IN THIS PLACE THAT FADES, THIS MOMENT THAT DIES BEFORE US.

UH-HUH. I COULD... REFER YOU TO ANOTHER *PRACTITIONER.* WE HAVE SOME VERY *GOOD* ONES HERE. *GRIMOIRE* MIGHT BE IDEAL.

OR, IF IT WOULD BE POSSIBLE TO...*WAIT* A FEW DAYS?

BY THEN, A BUNCH MORE E-MAIL HAD COME IN, AND I HAD TO SORT THROUGH IT, ANSWERING WHAT I COULD AND SAVING THE REST FOR KIM.

AND THINGS STAYED *QUIET* UNTIL...

UFF!

BACK!

BOSS! ARE YOU ALL RIGHT? YOU LOOK --

EXHAUSTED. AND *STARVING.*

BUT HERE -- THE *GUARDIAN RITUAL TEXTS.* ALL DONE, PROOFED, CORRECTED AND READY TO *GO.*

AND YOU WON'T HAVE TO WORRY ABOUT THAT *PAROLE CONSULTATION* FOR MR. MALEFIC.

HE *BROKE OUT* THIS AFTERNOON, AND I RAN INTO HIM FIGHTING *JACK-IN-THE-BOX* ON MY WAY HOME.

HOW YOU *DOING* IN THERE, MR. M?

CURSE YOU! CURSE YOU AND ALL YOU *KNOW,* FROM *THIS* GENERATION DOWN TO THE --

ORN, CAN YOU FIND OUR NEW FRIEND SPACE IN THE *BARN* FOR NOW? ASK WHAT HIS *NEEDS* ARE. I THINK HE CAN MAKE THEM KNOWN TO YOU.

GOMMP

SHE NEVER DID GET TO DELIVER *MR. MALEFIC*, NOT THAT DAY. I FILLED HER IN ON WHAT HAD HAPPENED AND ALL THE VARIOUS SCHEDULE CHANGES...

...AND WE WENT OVER THE REMAINING E-MAIL, STUFF SHE COULD TELL ME HOW TO ANSWER AND STUFF SHE'D HAVE TO HANDLE *HERSELF*.

AND MAY YOUR FEET BE COVERED IN BLISTERS, AND YOUR TOENAILS CUT TOO SHORT, AND YOUR LIPS BE ETERNALLY CHAPPED, AND YOUR --

AND *EVENTUALLY*...

BING BONG

THAT'LL BE *BELLAIRE* AND *DOREEN*. OKAY IF I KNOCK OFF NOW?

SURE, *SURE.* HEY, TONIGHT'S YOUR *GALLERY SHOW,* ISN'T IT?

JUST A COUPLE OF PIECES. IT'S A *GROUP* SHOW.

WHAT *TIME?* I'LL DROP BY -- I'M DYING TO *SEE* IT!

YOU DON'T NEED TO...

HEY, I *WANT* TO! AS SOON AS I'M DONE WITH THE *E-MAIL* HERE...

AND THE *PHONE CALLS*, AND A *PURIFYING RITUAL*, AND A CHAT WITH THE *TRANQUILITY FROG*, AND...

I'LL MAKE IT IF I *CAN*, OKAY?

SOUNDS *GREAT*.

BEL! DORY!

ANYTHING *WILD* HAPPEN TODAY?

THEY START TO ANSWER, AND I LISTEN. BUT THEY WEREN'T WHO I WAS *REALLY* ASKING...

FOUR ATTEMPTED *INCURSIONS*. ALL REPELLED BY THE BOYS AND ME. NONE SINCE THAT...*NEW THING* ARRIVED, WHATEVER IT IS. IT'LL BE A BIG HELP.

...ADVENTURE *AWAITS!*

YOU?

HA!

AND SHE *DID* SAY SHE OWED ME. MAYBE IF SHE DOES SHOW UP, WE CAN HIT THAT *SUSHI PLACE* SHE WAS TALKING ABOUT THIS MORNING.

I HAD AN EVENTFUL DAY. *HECTIC*, EVEN. BUT NOTHING I COULDN'T HANDLE.

NO, NOTHING I COULDN'T *HANDLE*.

SO *COME ON*, THEN...

I LOVE GOOD SUSHI.

YOU ARE NOW LEAVING
ASTRO CITY
PLEASE DRIVE CAREFULLY

When I was a LITTLE BOY, my favorite fairy tale was "Little Red Riding Hood."

Everything but the ENDING.

It wasn't LITTLE RED I liked it for. Silly, brainless girl, trip-trapping off through the dark woods without a thought in her head.

It wasn't GRANDMA, that timorous, twittering old biddy.

And it certainly wasn't the WOODSMAN. He was barely even a CHARACTER. Just someone to barge in at the end with an AXE, to tack on a "happy ending."

IDIOTS, the bunch of them.

The one I liked was the WOLF.

The Wolf was EVERYTHING I wanted to be.

He was CONFIDENT. He was CRAFTY. He wasn't scared of the woods. He was WHY the woods were scary.

The Wolf was SLY, slick, DANGEROUS. And most of all...

AH-AH! OUT IN THE *MIDDLE*, PLEASE, NO SILENT ALARMS...

CAME IN A LITTLE *EARLY* THERE, NED.

≶PFF≷ YOU CAME IN LATE, REGGIE, LIKE YOU SO OFTEN DO. *AND* A TAD FLAT.

NOW *NOW*, BOYS. I'M SURE NO ONE COULD *TELL*.

Yes. STYLE.

Let me INTRODUCE myself. I'm Edward James Carroway. "Ned" to my friends.

Or at least, that's my PROFESSIONAL name. I'm what they call a --

-- I WAS what they call a "clotheshorse." A COSTUMED CRIMINAL, one known for wearing distinctive, EXPENSIVE clothing.

I was a GOOD one, too.

But I never did it for the MONEY. Not really.

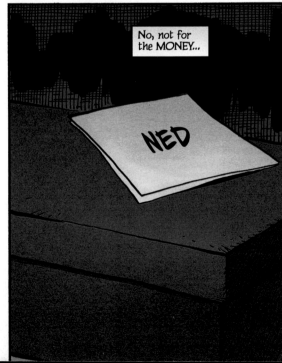

No, not for the MONEY...

NED

I was born Fred Glosman. Not even "Alfred." FRED. That's as much as my parents could THINK of.

I grew up in the SWEATSHOP. And not one of the nicer parts. No money. My father didn't WORK often enough for that.

Most of my clothes came from GOODWILL.

HA! AIN'T THAT MY OLD SHIRT? WE DITCHED IT WHEN IT GOT BARF ON IT!

OOOOOO, BARFO!

The other kids let me know what they THOUGHT of that.

I can't say I DISAGREED with them.

OTHER people didn't live that way.

OTHER people had nice clothes, nice things.

Nobody laughed at THEM, or called them "Stinky."

I wanted to be just like THEM.

HEY! HEY, KID! GET AWAY FROM THERE! YOU'LL SMEAR MY WINDOWS, YOU GRUBBY --

But I WASN'T.

I was like...mud. UGLY mud.

I had his WALLET. His address. His KEYS.

He'd been out for the EVENING. It'd be HOURS before anyone missed him.

I took over $1200, some expensive WATCHES, cufflinks and three more SUITS out of his apartment.

AND his appointment book.

All his FRIENDS' addresses. And most of the PARTIES and FUNCTIONS the gang'd be at, the next three months.

Nobody STOPPED me going in.

I looked RIGHT, after all. Looked like I BELONGED.

And on the way OUT...

...just in case any ALARMS had been set off...

And it was the beginning of an EDUCATION, too.

I learned that SHOES were the foundation. That in a truly FINE pair of shoes, you felt like you could take on the WORLD.

PERHAPS SOMETHING ITALIAN? *HANDMADE*, OF COURSE.

OH, OF COURSE.

All those CLOSETS. Those CLOTHES -- a wonderful, fascinating mystery, a new LANGUAGE to learn --

Like anything you DID was dancing.

And clothes -- FABRICS, summer and winter WEIGHTS, styles --

When a PLEAT is the perfect touch --

When a pocket square is OVERSTATEMENT --

Mm. *FAR* TOO COSTUMEY.

Doing research, I began to get IDEAS. For what became the ADELINES, and others.

I was in HEAVEN.

The right ENSEMBLE, made with skill and artistry -- it's like the body of a LOVER --

And SPEAKING of lovers --

She seemed so DELICATE. So vulnerable. Like she held UNIMAGINABLE secrets.

Her name was ALICE.

It was such a CHANGE, from before I'd become the Bandit. To feel CONFIDENT. In charge.

CHARMING.

I was the WOLF, and she was my prey. At least at FIRST.

I charmed her and BEGUILED her. Drew her in, making her helplessly, UTTERLY mine, in my POWER --

-- until one day I discovered I was the one who was lost. And she, with her fragile SMILE and her secret STRENGTHS --

She'd captured my HEART.

And I KNEW. From that day on, we'd live HAPPILY EVER --

BIRO ISLAND
PENITENTIARY

46

It was HARD. I felt like MUD again. Like a shapeless, formless, WORTHLESS THING.

Not worthy of HER. Not worthy of ANYONE.

But I HAD to be. For her. For the BABY on the way...

MAYBE...

YOU LIKE CLOTHES. MAYBE A JOB WORKING WITH NICE CLOTHES? OR WEARING THEM? IN A TAILOR SHOP, LIKE I USED TO? OR A THEATER USHER?

It was a FINE IDEA.

I grabbed a chance to sub for a SICK FRIEND. Didn't wear anything too fancy. Good SHOES. A well-cut shirt.

They were eating out of my HAND.

I caught people's ATTENTION. Moved from restaurant to restaurant. To better and BETTER jobs.

To a HEADWAITER gig, at Goscinny's --

THIS WAY, SENATOR.

YOUR REGULAR TABLE, OF COURSE.

But --

But something wasn't RIGHT --

I was charming. I was stylish. I SHOULD have felt good. But --

I found myself flinching at SHADOWS. Wanting to HIDE --

...AND SHE TOOK her BASKET, FULL OF WONDERFUL GOODIES...

...AND WENT SKIPPING OFF ALONG THE PATH THROUGH THE DEEP DARK WOODS, THAT LED TO GRANDMOTHER'S HOUSE...

But I wasn't the WOLF, was I?

The wolf was DANGEROUS. The wolf was in CONTROL.

The wolf didn't take TIPS!

My wolfing days were OVER, I told myself. I'd just have to get USED to it. There was ALICE to think about. And little JILL.

It was around then that I got an E-MAIL...

COLIN?

In prison, there'd been OTHERS like me. FASHION PLATES, they called us. DAPPER DANS. CLOTHESHORSES.

COLIN PEPPER was one of them. He could make PRISON BAGGIES look crisp. OSCAR HIJUEROS. Eddie Barnett. CHARLIE ZIMMER.

The other cons thought we must all be GAY.

And some of us WERE, sure, but maybe not as many as you'd think.

It was just a pleasure to talk to others who UNDERSTOOD. To feel like you weren't ALONE.

THE GRIST MILL? 10:30?

And Colin was getting some of us TOGETHER.

Just to have a few DRINKS.

Talk FABRICS and TAILORING with someone whose eyes didn't glaze over.

What could it HURT?

It was SUCH a relief.

The FEEL of a well-turned cuff. The FEAR in their eyes.

I felt it in my teeth. In my CANINES.

I told Alice it was a SPECIAL GIG -- a very exclusive PRIVATE PARTY. If I did well, a whole LUCRATIVE CIRCUIT of them.

But I was CAREFUL. I didn't stay with any group LONG, didn't set any patterns.

I worked with the GATSBYS --

With the MOUNT RUSHMORE FOUR and others --

I even subbed in for one of the long-running MENAGERIE GANG -- for the WOLF, of course --

-- and I'm proud to say I was the one who FINALLY talked them out of those awful JUMPSUITS.

And now here I AM.

The walls in this place practically SWEAT, and the carpets smell like something DIED on them. Probably DID.

I work in COVERALLS. With grime and grease. With RAGS.

My parole officer wouldn't THINK of letting me anywhere near a job involving a tuxedo.

And he's RIGHT, he's right.

I'm NEVER going to win back Alice. But if there's the tiniest chance, the barest HINT of one...I've GOT to change. I've got to be GOOD.

To be STRONG.

NED

He'd been known by many names, in many lands, since the dawn of all things. Al~la~lil~il, the Morning Brother. Xitu of the Evening Light. The Nurturer. The Spark~Blower. The Robed God. Pendifisciarni, the Fisher of Hearts. A thousand thousand names, uttered by a million million lips, in hope, prayer, desperation, joy.

But the name he felt most suited him, the name he thought of as himself, rather than a mere symbol of himself, was the **Dancing Master**.

He was the Dancing Master. An instructor. A commander. An opener of hearts.

It was he, after all, who caused Terem to dream of Talami, and cross oceans of fire to find her. It was he who set a blaze in the soul of Marandra of Teth, who carved out an empire in her love for Beredil. It was he who the slim youth of Deptu prayed to, at first hair and first blood, that they might find their other~own.

It was he who taught the stars to dance, so long and long ago.

It was he who taught merriment, and the sweet pain of yearning.

He was the Dancing Master. He had been called.

And he was here.

Waltz of the Hours

5:00 AM

R&D UNIT 7, ROUTCAULT CAMPUS, N.R. GISTICS INC.

EVER SINCE *ED NICHOLLS* AND *DAVISON ROYCE* HAD DISCOVERED THE *N-FIELD*, BACK IN THE 1950s, IT HAD BEEN A FASCINATING MYSTERY.

HOW DID SIGNALS TRANSMIT THROUGH THE FIELD IN APPARENT *VIOLATION* OF ANY KNOWN PHYSICS?

AND NOW --

THE ROBOT WAS ON *IO*, IN ORBIT AROUND *JUPITER*.

THE SIGNALS -- THEY'RE *FINALLY* SEEING SOME DELAY. OR IS IT JUST *DEGRADATION?* IS IT TIME, DISTANCE OR --

GOT IT, GOT IT, GOT IT GOT IT GOT --

DAMMIT! DROPPED THE *SAMPLE!*

DEFINITE FLUCTUATION IN COMMAND FLOW.

BUT *VIDEO* IS UNINTERRUPTED. STILL COMING THROUGH THE INSTA-LINK CLEAN AND --

WHO'S CUSPING? BROUGHT YOU *COFFEE.* CHUCK, ALLISON, HERACLIO, THE *CAVALRY'S* HERE.

ZVI!

YOU CAN MAKE THIS DAMNED RIG WORK. I'M *OUTTA* HERE!

9:00 AM

ASTROBANK, KREMER STREET BRANCH. DERBYVILLE.

SHE'S GOING TO BREAK UP WITH HIM. THAT MUCH, AT LEAST, SHE KNOWS.

WHEN SHE FIRST MOVED TO THE CITY, IT FELT GREAT. SO MUCH POSSIBILITY. EXCITEMENT, ROMANCE. IT WAS THRILLING.

BUT NOW?

ALL SHE DOES IS HANDLE MONEY THAT ISN'T HERS. AND FAKE-SMILE AT PEOPLE WHO ARE FED UP WITH WAITING IN LINE.

HERE YOU GO.

3.8% financing

AND HER SO-CALLED BOYFRIEND? WHEN DOES SHE SEE HIM?

JUST BAD TIMING, HE SAYS. WORK, HE SAYS. HE WISHES THEY COULD, HE SAYS. IS HE SEEING SOMEONE ELSE?

MAYBE SHE JUST NEEDS TO GET OUT. A NEW START. NEW PLACE. BY THE OCEAN SOMEWHERE.

SHE LIKES THE OCEAN.

NEXT?

1:00 AM

THE PLUNKETT-WINSOR FACILITY FOR EXPERIMENTAL PHYSICS, FOX-BROOME UNIVERSITY.

DAY 113 OF TEST READINGS. NIGHT 113, ACTUALLY.

THE APPARATUS HAS TO BE *MONITORED*, BUT RARELY *ADJUSTED*. IF IT'S GOING TO *BREAK THROUGH* -- GOING TO FIND THE THEORIZED *"DIMENSIONAL PINHOLES"* --

-- IT'S JUST A MATTER OF CYCLING THROUGH COMBINATIONS OF *STIMULI* AND *SUBQUARK FREQUENCY*, AND ANY TIME THE FIELD READINGS *"DIMPLE"* --

-- BARRAGING THE *AETHERIC* WITH DIGITIZED MANDELBROT PROBES.

RIGHT.

THAT'S WHEN MOST VISITING BIGWIGS' *EYES* START TO *GLAZE OVER*. IT'S *SIMPLE*, BUT NOT EXACTLY EASY TO EXPLAIN.

STILL, IT REQUIRES 24-HOUR MONITORING. *LIVE* MONITORING. AND THEY HAVE SUCH A *TINY BUDGET* --

Da da d-d-*da* da, da dee-dee da *dum...*

HE'D GOTTEN THE *STROGANOFF* RECIPE FROM MOM. SHE WAS FINE. DAD WAS FINE. HE WAS UP TO 18TH-LEVEL PALADIN IN *WAYCRAFTER*.

FIVE HOURS TO GO.

FIVE HOURS, AND THEN *HOME*. AND STILL NO REAL HUMAN CONTACT. A COLD BED, MAYBE A *NOTE* ON THE FRIDGE.

TENDERNESS *DEFERRED*. A CARESS BY *PROXY*.

It had been long indeed. Longer than he'd known.

These towers rivaled the spires of Talla~Le. In height, at least, though never in beauty. And the avenues, so long and peopled~

Where did such multitudes come from? Were they all the men and women of the world? But no~the Dancing Master could sense that the numbers only went on and on, girdling the world, like veli~bugs on rotten moonfruit. So many!

And in their thoughts, such heaviness. A spark here and there, a song trilled hesitantly in a bedchamber or a market stall. A deeper hum, in corners and crannies. The dance, it was still within them.

But so many had thoughts only of resentment, or a despair so old it had grown dull and familiar. There was anger and pain. And loneliness, deep wells of it. Against that, the flicker of the dance was so slight, so frail, that one might think it could be swallowed up entirely.

It had been long. Too long, perhaps...?

The Dance.

They ache so, for the Dance...

2:00 PM

AH, LAURA? PLEASE, DON'T...

WHAT IS SHE DOING?!

HE LEFT, WITHOUT TAKING ANYTHING.

HE CAME BACK.

HE GAVE HER THE GUNS AND TOLD HER TO *COVER* THEM.

HE LEFT AGAIN.

SHE SHOULD GET *DOWN.* CALL THE POLICE, HIT THE ALARM --

BUT -- BUT --

THAT *SMILE.* SOMETHING IN HIS EYES.

THERE'S SOMETHING -- SOMETHING --

HEY. ATTAGIRL.

HERE. EVERYTHING I TOOK THIS MORNING. *THREE BANKS'* WORTH. TELL THE COPS *THEY* CAN SORT IT OUT. I'M RETIRED.

YOU AN' *ME.* LET'S BOO-BOO.

This world. It had been long since he had been here. Long and long again. He felt it, strange and different. All around him, pulsing with life and dreams and the driving rhythm of beating hearts. It was changing him. He could feel it. As he could change it.

It was not what he had been called for...

No. No, it was not.

But it would surely not hurt to see...

HEY, *LOOK.* YOU KNOW THE DRILL. THAT'S REAL *N* --

HEY.

UM. HEY?

WHERE YOU *BEEN* ALL MY LIFE?

I, UM...

IOWA? MOSTLY?

6:00 AM

HOW'S THINGS AT *HOME*?

OH, YOU KNOW. *SCHEDULES.* IT'S HARD, BUT WE'LL MAKE IT.

YOU *SURE?* NO OFFENSE, BUT YOU'RE LOOKING TIRED. TIRED AND *SAD.* YOU NEED A VACATION, BOTH OF --

CAN'T RIGHT NOW, JENELLE. YOU KNOW HOW IT IS.

IT'S A BITCH AND A *HALF,* BUT THERE'S NO WAY AROUND -- *HEY!*

LOOK! LOOK, I GOT IT!

I MULTI-*SHEATHED* THE N-TUNNEL, AND THE DEGRADATION *VANISHED.* I DIDN'T *THINK* IT WAS DISTANCE. IT'S SOMETHING IN THE N-FIELD *ITSELF* --

I BET YOU'RE *RIGHT.* OH, THIS IS *HUGE,* ZVI.

I'M GOING TO GO GET *ABERNATHY.* HE'S GOT TO SEE THIS. THIS IS *GOOD,* REALLY GOOD --

LOOK, LOOK --

HE COULD *CALL.* IT'S A BREAKTHROUGH, IT'S WORTH *SHARING,* HE COULD CALL.

BUT THEY *AGREED.* THEY BOTH WERE SO SHORT ON SLEEP THESE DAYS. IT WASN'T FOREVER. IT'D *END.* BUT IT WAS SO -- SO HARD TO --

KBAC NEWS — CITY LIVE REPORT

-- WAVE OF INCIDENTS IN THE CITY CENTER, A "ROMANTIC PLAGUE," IF YOU WILL. CITIZENS ARE URGED TO STAY AWAY, THOUGH THE EFFECT MAY BE SPREADING.

THE FIRST REPORTS CAME IN SHORTLY AFTER 8 AM --

SHE WANTS TO CALL HOME. TO TALK TO HER HUSBAND.

TO SEE IF HE KNOWS ANYTHING, A LITTLE. TO SEE HOW THE KIDS ARE DOING, EVEN MORE. TO HEAR HIS VOICE, TO THINK OF HIS ARMS, HIS LAUGH, HIS --

KBAC 3 — BREAKING NEWS ▷▷▷ — DOWNTOWN GRIDLOCKED

-- ABANDONED CARS, CLOSED BUSINESSES, EVEN EMPTY OFFICES.

MULTIPLE REPORTS OF SPONTANEOUS DANCING, OF PICNICS, OF DEEP, CONFESSIONAL CONVERSATIONS WITH NEAR-STRANGERS, AND ACTS OF A MORE PRIVATE NATURE --

HE NEEDS TO GET TO A PHONE.

ANGIE McTIERNEY. WHAT THEY'D HAD IN COLLEGE -- HOW COULD HE HAVE LET IT SLIP AWAY? THEY'VE EXCHANGED CHRISTMAS CARDS, BUT --

-- AND FOR AN ON-THE-SPOT REPORT, WE SWITCH YOU TO --

PETEY? IS ANYONE THERE?

VALERIE? LLOYD?

THE **MICRO-CANNON** ACTIVATE, AS THEY'RE PROGRAMMED TO.

THE AIR IS FULL OF SUBATOMIC **ENERGY MODULATION,** **PLASMIC CHORD PATTERNS** AND **BATCH-PACKETS** OF SYLLABIC MATH.

IT **SHOULD** BE, PERHAPS, FINE-TUNED BASED ON THE RESPONSES TO THE **MANDELBROT PULSES** --

BUT INSTEAD --

INSTEAD, THERE'S **SOMETHING ELSE** IN THE AIR. SOMETHING INTANGIBLE, SOMETHING UNINTENDED.

SOMETHING PROJECTED BY **NO MACHINE.**

SOMETHING THAT BESEECHES --

It had not been too long. The Dance was still within them. But the Dancing Master—as he hummed the lost chords and saw sparks flicker to the beginnings of flame—was joined by another.

The Dark One. Tereth~Il, he'd been called once, and Kerem the Wise. And a hundred other names. And now he wore a sack upon his head and told the Dancing Master he must leave.

"I do no harm," the Dancing Master said. "I bring pleasure and awakening, a joy in life long missed by these stunted ones. No one acts against their nature, or against their heart."

"Your music has been too long gone," said the Hanged Man, for as such he was known here and now, "and it is too strong. It overwhelms them.

"Already you disrupt their world. Let them go, merry courtier. Let them think you a form of temporary madness, before your music upsets their whole world."

And the Dancing Master knew it was the truth. They felt joy, some of them. But they felt the stirrings of fear, as well, as they wondered what swept their truths, their hearts, into the open.

"The Old Lands are cold," said the Dancing Master. "Dull, and empty, and we are all so tiring there."

"I know," said the Hanged Man. "But still, you must go."

"Very well," said the Dancing Master. "I go. But there is a thing I must do first. "I was beseeched. I came. And I must serve he who called me."

HA!

GREAT! GREAT!

THREE LEVELS OF N-TUNNEL SHEATHING, AND THERE'S ALMOST NO MEASURABLE INTERFERENCE AT ALL! LOOK AT IT GO!

A FEW MORE HOURS OF CALIBRATION, AND WE SHOULD BE ABLE TO --

YOU OKAY?

YEAH. YEAH, I'M JUST --

I'M --

AND I JUST DON'T KNOW WHAT CAME *OVER* ME. BUT I KNEW I WANTED A DIFFERENT LIFE, A MORE *SETTLED* LIFE. AND I WANTED IT WITH *YOU.*

I KNOW. IT WAS LIKE -- A *LIGHT* COMING ON, WASN'T IT?

A LIGHT. OR *MUSIC,* MAYBE.

I LIKE YOUR *REAL VOICE,* BY THE WAY. WAY BETTER THAN THAT MOUNTAIN-BOY THING. BUT I DON'T -- WHERE ARE YOU *FROM?*

MAINE. I'M FROM *MAINE.*

I WAS THINKING. MY GREAT-UNCLE -- HE'S GOT NO *KIDS,* AND HE'S GOT THIS *LOBSTER JOINT* ON THE COAST, UP NEAR ROCKLAND.

HE BUGS ME TO COME *RUN* IT WITH HIM.

YOU LIKE *LOBSTER?*

ARE YOU KIDDING? I *LOVE* LOBSTER...

It was good. That which he was called for. It was strong. It had value. It would be good.

And there were sparks. Sparks that had known the breath of life. Would they all take flame? Surely not. Some would fizzle and darken. But some would kindle.

Some would burn long. Some would burn a lifetime.

This world. He could change it. It would change him. It already had. Would that be so bad? Would it not be~

~for he knew the way back, now~

But no. The memory of the day~the sparks about to kindle, the tinder about to flame~

It would have to keep him warm, there in the Old Lands. It would have to~

MIDNIGHT

HAS ANYONE REACHED JIM YET? WHEN YOU *DO*, TELL HIM TO GET HIS ASS --

IT'S *OKAY*, PETE. ROVER'S JUST CYCLING THROUGH TESTS. IT'S BEEN A *CRAZY DAY* OUT THERE, SO LET'S JUST CUT EVERYONE SOME SLACK --

"-- AND FOCUS ON GETTING BACK TO *NORMAL*."

ROVER. ITS NAME IS ROVER.

ITS NAME IS ROVER AND THIS IS IO AND IT DOESN'T HEAR JIM'S VOICE AND IT DOESN'T HEAR ZVI'S VOICE AND IT'S *ALL ALONE*.

IT DOESN'T KNOW HOW IT KNOWS *ANY* OF THIS. BUT IT KNOWS IT.

ITS NAME IS ROVER AND THE MUSIC WENT RIGHT *THROUGH* IT --

AND JIM AND ZVI AND CHUCK ARE ALL GONE AND IT WANTS THEM *BACK*.

IT WANTS THE MUSIC BACK.

YOU ARE NOW LEAVING **ASTRO CITY** PLEASE DRIVE CAREFULLY

...AND THIS FELLOW *HERE*, OH MY, *HE* HAD A LIVELY TIME OF IT.

YOU CAN SEE THE *SCARS* HE ACCUMULATED OVER THE YEARS. GREGORY WAS A *FIGHTER*, RIGHT TO THE END. *WEREN'T* YOU, GREGORY?

AND NOW OVER *HERE* IS A REAL FAVORITE...

YOU -- YOU TALK ABOUT THEM AS IF THEY'RE *OLD FRIENDS*.

OH, *YES*, YES. WHY *WOULDN'T* I? AFTER ALL...

I TAKE THEM THROUGH THE HIGH POINTS.

MECHIZMO'S BATTLES WITH THE OMEGA RANGERS, THAT'S ALWAYS POPULAR...

THE BALL-BEARIANS...

THE ROBO-KILLERS. BUT I CALL THEM THE ROBO-CALLERS. WHAT AN AWFUL NAME TO GIVE TO A POOR MACHINE...

...AND WE FINISH UP WITH ARTHUR HERE. THE LAST KNOWN SCANDROID TO ESCAPE DESTRUCTION, I BELIEVE.

I DO HAVE COOKIES, IN THE SHED. AND ICED TEA. FOR SALE, I'M AFRAID, BUT --

THAT'S OKAY. WE HAVE TO RUN. BUT THIS WAS REALLY FASCINATING, MS...?

ELLIE. JUST ELLIE.

THEY DO SEEM TO HAVE LIKED IT. THE YOUNG MAN ESPECIALLY.

DO COME BACK, IF YOU CAN. THERE'S LOTS MORE -- I ONLY SHOWED YOU THE BASICS --

OH, WE WILL, IF WE CAN. AND WE'LL TELL OUR FRIENDS. I CAN'T BELIEVE THIS PLACE ISN'T BETTER KNOWN...

SUCH A NICE FAMILY.

THAT'S NINE TODAY, VERY GOOD FOR AUGUST. AND THAT ONE GROUP THIS MORNING -- SHE'D COME AS A CHILD, AND NOW WANTED TO SHOW IT TO HER CHILDREN.

SO SWEET.

IT HAS BEEN A LONG TIME, HASN'T IT? SO LONG SINCE --

I WAS -- WAS --

NO, ELLIE. NO, YOU OLD FOOL! DON'T THINK ABOUT THAT, NOT THOSE DAYS. NEVER THOSE DAYS --

I HEARD ABOUT IT. HEARD SOMEHOW --

AND I COULDN'T -- I COULDN'T LEAVE IT ALONE. COULDN'T LET IT GO.

I JUST THOUGHT -- ABOUT HOW SCARED THEY MUST BE, TO BE HURT LIKE THAT, WITH NO ONE TO COME FOR THEM. NO ONE TO END THEIR TORMENT.

THEY'D BEEN ABANDONED -- FORGOTTEN WHEN SHE REVERTED THE HEROES AND A LOT OF OTHERS INTO CHILDREN, TEMPORARILY --

-- AND I WAS RIGHT. NO ONE HAD THOUGHT TO RESCUE THEM --

OH...

BIP BIP bip BIP

IT'S OKAY, LITTLE ONE.

I'M HERE, I'M HERE. YOU'LL BE ALL RIGHT...

SO *LONG AGO*, IT WAS. AND NOW -- IT'S SO *NICE* HERE. SO PEACEFUL, SO QUIET. SO *SAFE*.

SEVENTEEN CYBERWINGS, I SAVED. AND REPAIRED *SIX* OF THEM, OR MOSTLY. NOT A MUSEUM, THEN. NOT WITH JUST ONE *SET*.

BUT IT WAS A *START*, WASN'T IT? A START.

LOOKS LIKE VISITORS WERE *GENEROUS* TODAY. THEY LIKE THE *STORIES*, LIKE HEARING ABOUT WHAT *HAPPENED*.

THAT'S WHAT MAKES IT *LIVE*.

MM. TWENTY-FIVE, FORTY-FIVE, FIFTY...

I CAN GO TO THE *GROCERY* TONIGHT.

PASTA, CHEESE, SOME OF THAT NICE GRANOLA WITH THE PECANS, MMM. AND FOR THEM. *METAL* POLISH. A NEW *FAULT* SENSOR.

AND MAYBE AN *IONIC* --

HM?

WHO -- ?

95

BUT WHEN YOU FOUND THE RIGHT WAY TO *HANDLE* THEM --

YOU'D MADE A FRIEND. A *GOOD* FRIEND. FOR LIFE. AND I'D MADE SO MANY FRIENDS. *MORE* THAN FRIENDS...

tik SYSTEMS ONLINE...TARGET DETECTED...

ACTIVATING WEAPONRY...

VMMMM...

NO, NO, WE CAN'T HAVE *THAT.* LET'S TAKE A...

AH! TOO FEW RESPONSE PATHWAYS!

BZT ZZZT

WEAPON... WEAPONRY...

THAT'S SO *SAD.* BUT WE CAN GIVE YOU MORE *OPTIONS.* WOULDN'T YOU LIKE THAT?

I *BET* YOU'D LIKE THAT...

ROBO ROBO ROBOT ACTION TOY

NOW. *STILL* WANT YOUR WEAPONRY?

I-LIKE-TO-FROLIC-AND-PLAY! SEE-MY-TAIL-WAG!

OH, *NO,* NO. FAR TOO MUCH, *FAR* TOO MUCH...

YOU *KNOW,* AUNT ELLIE... I'M NOT SURE YOU FULLY *REALIZE* WHAT YOU'VE GOT HERE...

I KEEP BODY AND SOUL *TOGETHER.* AND I'VE GOT MY FRIENDS.

WHAT MORE WOULD I *NEED?*

robot MUSEUM

An Incredible Gallery of Fantastic Fo[?]s!

ENTRANCE →

HMP.

SORRY, PAL, TIMES ARE TOUGH ALL OVER.

$30 Per Carload

CAN'T SURVIVE ON *DONATIONS* ANY MORE.

MUSEUM →

UH, I THINK THAT ONE'S CALLED *"CANNONADE."* WORKED FOR... THE *IRON COLONEL?*

WE'LL HAVE A BROCHURE TO SELL IN THE *GIFT SHOP,* IT'S AT THE PRINTER.

SELF-GUIDED *AUDIO TOUR,* TOO. REAL SOON NOW.

OH, IT ALL LOOKS SO *NICE!* ARE WE GETTING MORE VISITORS?

WELL, NOT JUST *YET.* THERE'S ALWAYS A *LAG,* ADJUSTMENT TO NEW CHANGES. WE'LL DO *FINE,* YOU'LL SEE.

885·PPR

BUT THE *MUSEUM.* THE STORIES, THEY'RE SO IMPORTANT.

WE CAN GO *OVER* THEM AGAIN...

THEY'RE *IMPORTANT,* YES.

BUT SO ARE NEW EXHIBITS. NEW *ATTRACTIONS.* THE STUFF YOU'RE COLLECTING, FINDING NEW *ROBOTS,* THAT'S CRUCIAL.

101

-- DARING ROBBERY AT THE *KREMER TOWERS,* CAUGHT HERE ON SECURITY-CAM FOOTAGE --

OH DEAR,, OH DEAR. SKUTTLEBUGS.

I DIDN'T *KNOW* THERE WERE ANY OTHER SURVIVING SKUTTLEBUGS, EXCEPT FOR THE ONES HERE AT --

HAIL, THE CONQUERING HERO!

I BRING *BEER!* AND *RIBEYES!* WE FEAST TONIGHT!

WE'VE BEEN STARTING TO *DO BETTER,* AUNT ELLIE, SO I FIGURED IT WAS TIME I PULLED MY *WEIGHT* A LITTLE, SHOPPING-WISE!

OH!

HOPE YOU DON'T MIND ME BORROWING THE *SCOOTER...*

NO, NO, OF *COURSE* NOT!

IT'S *NICE,* HAVING ANOTHER PERSON HERE -- ANOTHER *HUMAN.*

BUT THEN, I'VE NEVER *REALLY* BEEN ALONE...

WHAT DO *YOU* THINK, ARTHUR?

MEEP!

...NOT SINCE I STARTED THE *MUSEUM.*

MUSEUM THIS WAY

WE CAN *DO* THIS. WE'RE ALL AGREED? WE *CAN* DO IT...

AT FIRST, I THOUGHT IT WAS JUST A WAY TO AFFORD *FOOD* -- AND SUPPLIES TO REPAIR MORE *ROBOTS.*

BUT WHAT IT *BECAME* -- I'VE HAD SUCH GOOD TIMES --

JIMMY? JIMMY **SHADE!** LISTEN TO ME.

YOU'VE GOT TO COHERE **SLOWLY** -- JUST YOUR **HAND,** SO WE CAN PULL YOU OUT. **MEDULLA,** KEEP HIM CALM, KEEP HIM FOCUSED...

THE KONTROLLERS **ESCAPED,** BUT --

...SO **AWFUL,** BEING USED LIKE THAT. KONTROLLER PROCESSORS, THEY'RE **SO** SENSITIVE. I JUST **KNOW** THEY FEEL SUCH GUILT AT BEING FORCED TO...HMP. **HMPH!**

FRED! FRED, DEAR, CAN YOU HELP ME WITH --

AUNT ELLIE! YOU'RE JUST IN **TIME!**

WE'VE BEEN DOING **SO WELL,** I THOUGHT A CELEBRATION WAS IN ORDER...

WH...?

BUT -- BUT I THOUGHT WE WERE STILL WAITING -- THE **LAG,** YOU'D SAID!

I NEVER SEE **CARS** IN THE PARKING AREA, AND THE DAYS I STAY **HOME** --

AW, IT'S **TRAFFIC PATTERNS,** REALLY. TOUR GROUPS, SCHOOLS -- WE'RE **CONCENTRATING** THE ATTENDANCE, FOR NOW.

SMALLER WINDOW, GREATER **USAGE?**

OH? I... SUPPOSE THAT MAKES SENSE, THEN...

HE'D BEEN MAKING A CHARITY APPEARANCE -- CHARITY!

RAISING MONEY FOR SICK CHILDREN!

SAMARITAN --

ARAÖW!

BUT WORSE --

Friends & Relations

WRAKKk

IN THE END, HE SAYS SOMETHING ABOUT HOW I'M *MALINGERING.* WHICH IS NONSENSE, I'M HEALTHY AS AN *OLD HORSE.*

ANY WORD ON RECORDS, BILL? I NEED *SOMETHING* TO WORK WITH HERE... ...AND ALL SHE DOES IS NATTER ON ABOUT HER *"FRIENDS"...*

WE *WISH.* NO FINGERPRINT RECORDS. NO DNA MATCH.

SHE'S JUST NOT IN THE *SYSTEM.* AS FAR AS WE CAN TELL, *"ELLIE JIMSON"* HAS NEVER *VOTED,* NEVER HELD A DRIVER'S LICENSE, *NOTHING.*

OH, GREAT.

IT'S LIKE SHE'S A *GHOST.* LIKE SHE NEVER EXISTED. EITHER SHE'S *WAAAAY* MORE DEVIOUS THAN SHE LOOKS...

THEY TELL ME THERE'LL BE *ANOTHER HEARING,* AND I HAVE TO STAY FOR *THAT,* TOO.

AS IF I HAVE THE TIME TO JUST *WAIT AROUND...*

...OR SOMETHING *SERIOUSLY SCREWY* IS GOING ON HERE...

I DON'T *LIKE* IT. THEY WON'T LET ME GO, AND MY FRIENDS ARE IN TROUBLE.

THEY WON'T LET ME *GO* --

-- AND I *CAN'T* -- I CAN'T --

YOU *UNDERSTAND,* ELLIE. DON'T YOU?

YOU -- YOU --

IT *HAS* TO BE THIS WAY.

IT *HAS* TO BE.

B-BUT I HAVE TO *FIGHT* THE MEMORIES. HOLD THEM BACK.

MY FRIENDS ARE IN *TROUBLE.* THEY NEED ME.

THE DANGER ISN'T *OVER.*

119

YOU THOUGHT YOU'D MAKE THE MUSEUM A *SUCCESS.* AND WHEN IT DIDN'T WORK RIGHT AWAY YOU DIDN'T ADMIT IT. YOU TOOK THE *EASY WAY* OUT.

YOU RENTED MY ROBOTS TO *CRIMINALS* WHEN I WAS OUT. AND CLAIMED THE MONEY WAS COMING FROM THE MUSEUM.

AND OF *COURSE* THEY TRACED THE ROBOTS RIGHT BACK HERE.

I SHOULDN'T HAVE LET THEM *BLAME* YOU. I SHOULD HAVE TOLD THEM --

BUT YOU'RE *WEAK,* FRED. YOU'VE *ALWAYS* BEEN WEAK. CAN'T MAKE A BUSINESS WORK, CAN'T MAKE A *MARRIAGE* WORK.

RAN THROUGH YOUR INHERITANCE LIKE *WATER.* AND IT'S ALWAYS SOMEONE *ELSE'S* FAULT, ISN'T IT?

PROPERTY OF BONLYN COUNTY

-- TOLD THEM IT WAS *ME.* BUT I --

I DON'T -- WHAT --

NO, IT -- HUH?

I SHOULD HAVE KNOWN. *MY* MISTAKE, I SUPPOSE. BUT YOU CAN'T UNBREAK A *WINDOW,* FRED. JUST LEARN NOT TO DO IT NEXT TIME. CAN YOU *DO* THAT?

I *CAN!* YOU'LL SEE, I'LL --

IT'S NOT *ME* THAT NEEDS TO SEE, DEAR. IT'S *YOU.* BUT WE'VE GOT THINGS TO DO. WHO *WAS* IT?

HUH?

THINGS *ESCALATED.* THE PEOPLE PAYING YOU.

POLICE LINE - D

PROPERTY OF BONLYN COUNTY

WHO *WAS* IT, AT THE END?

IT TURNS OUT VIVI HAD BEEN PLANTING CIRCUITRY IN ALL KINDS OF GOVERNMENT EQUIPMENT, FROM DMVs TO THE PENTAGON.

SHE'D BEEN DOING IT FOR YEARS, PART OF SOME CRAZY TAKEOVER PLAN. BUT IT WAS FULL OF AN OLD ROUTING CIRCUITRY I'D DESIGNED. SOME OF WHICH I'D USED IN REPAIRS.

SO WHEN FRED STARTED RENTING OUT MY BOYS, IT CREATED A RISK.

IF THEY'D FOUND IT IN MY ROBOTS, AND IT LED THEM TO HERS...

...GOING TO BE ALL RIGHT?

I'LL BE FINE.

TANGLED WEBS. SUCH VERY TANGLED WEBS WE BUILD OUT OF OBSESSION AND ANGER. CAN'T BE GOOD FOR THE BLOOD PRESSURE.

I STILL HAVE SOME MONEY -- PAYOFFS E.A.G.L.E. DIDN'T FIND, TO BE HONEST -- AND THAT'LL GET ME STARTED IN CHICAGO.

I WORRY ABOUT YOU, YOU KNOW.

SHE'D BEEN LOOKING FOR ME FOR YEARS, ANYWAY. I SUPPOSE FRED HELPED WITH THAT. SHE'S NOT ON MY TRAIL ANY MORE. FOR NOW, AT LEAST.

AUNT ELLIE, I GOT YOU FRAMED FOR ROBBERY, ASSAULT AND TERRORISM, AND NEARLY SENT YOU TO PRISON.

YES, YES. TAKING THE EASY WAY OUT. YOU HAVE TO STOP DOING THAT, YOU KNOW.

BZZ   BZZ

BZZ...

YOU ARE
NOW LEAVING
**ASTRO
CITY**
PLEASE D...
CAREFULLY

STILL *THERE*, RICK? IT'S DONE.

I CAN'T SAY IT WAS MUCH OF A *CHALLENGE*.

THAT WAS FAST.

...BUT AT LEAST IT WAS A *WILD* ONE.

HEY! IT -- IT WAS --

NO -- CAN'T BE --

LOOKED LIKE --

NOT REALLY THE KIND OF THING I'D EXPECT YOU TO HAVE *TROUBLE* WITH, NO.

BUT, AH -- DID YOU GO TO *SUPPORT GROUP* TODAY?

I'LL CALL YOU *BACK*, OKAY?

HEY, NO! COME ON *OVER*, AT LEAST! DON'T --

KLEK

"DON'T *WALLOW* IN IT." THAT'S WHAT HE WAS GOING TO SAY. HE'S SAID IT OFTEN ENOUGH *BEFORE*. BUT IT'S HARD NOT TO.

IT'S HARD TO SIT THROUGH THAT *SUPPORT GROUP*, TOO. IT HELPS, I KNOW. BUT THERE'S THINGS I CAN OPEN UP ABOUT, AND THINGS I *CAN'T*.

THAT MAKES IT...*TRICKY*.

HEY, **HEY!** BIG GAME, HUH? BLOOD PUMPING, SCHOOL HONOR ON THE LINE? EXCITING, ISN'T IT?

THIS IS *SIMON.* AND SIMON SAYS...

...PAY ATTENTION.

Simon Says. Our own home-grown supervillain. Or mad scientist. Or whatever the term was.

AW, MAN!

SIMON?

He hadn't made much noise in a while...

I HAVE A **MESSAGE** FOR YOU-KNOW-WHO.

TELL HIM I WANT TO **TALK.** I'LL MEET HIM ON TOP OF MOUNT POCKY AT 9:00 TONIGHT. IT'LL BE WORTH HIS WHILE -- IF HE CARES TO SHOW UP!

NOT THE **EASIEST** GUY TO GET AHOLD OF -- BUT I BET **THIS** LITTLE TRICK WILL CATCH HIS NOTICE, HMM?

AND **NOW,** I RETURN YOU TO YOUR **THRILLING** GAME --

Right then, no one cared about Simon Says. Or Starbright, or anything else. They just wanted the ball to go between the uprights. They just wanted the goal.

But if there was one thing everyone in town knew about Simon, it was this...

...Simon Says was a grade-A jerk.

Not that he didn't have reason. Especially when it came to the football team.

Simon Siezmanski. Smartest kid in town. Maybe the world. But he'd always been awkward. A little different, a little fey.

And a bunch of the jocks made a thing of it. Wanted him to know what they thought of him.

HA HA!

LOSER!

FAIRY!

HEY! SOMEONE DO SOMETH --

It was Chet Markham who cut him down. Even in seventh grade, a quarterback. One of the jocks.

EASY, SIMON. I'LL GET YOU LOOSE. AND WHOEVER DID THIS --

That can't have sat well.

GET AWAY!

YOU'RE ONE OF THEM! JUST ONE MORE! ALL OF YOU! ALL --

That was when he stopped even trying to fit in.

That was when he vanished, and came back as Simon Says. For revenge.

BDINT

And when Starbright heard what Simon wanted...

WHAT?!

SIMON, I'VE TOLD YOU, OVER AND OVER...IF I CAN *HELP* SOMEHOW, GET YOU TO *GIVE UP* YOUR CRAZY VENDETTA, I'LL DO IT IN A HEARTBEAT.

BUT *THIS* -- IF THIS IS A WAY TO STRIKE AT ME THROUGH MY *FRIENDS*...

THEY USED TO BE *YOUR* FRIENDS...

I *KNEW* YOU WOULDN'T BELIEVE ME. YOU *TALK* ABOUT TRUST, BUT YOU'RE JUST LIKE ALL THE *REST* OF THE WORLD.

YOU THINK I'M A FREAK WHO SHOULD BE *LOCKED UP.*

SO I CAME UP WITH A WAY TO *CONVINCE* YOU I'M IN EARNEST.

YOU KNOW YOUR *"HERO"* CRUSADE SICKENS ME. SAVING *MORONS* AND *THROWBACKS* WHO SHOULD DIE OFF TO IMPROVE THE SPECIES.

BUT I'LL *JOIN* YOU. TO GET WHAT I WANT -- I'LL HELP *YOU* FIGHT CRIME.

YOU'LL...?

A 24-HOUR *TRUCE.*

I SPEND TOMORROW HELPING YOU *TRACK DOWN* AND CAPTURE *CRIMINALS,* AND IN THE EVENING YOU DO AS I *ASK.*

24 HOURS. YOU GET TO USE THE BRILLIANT MIND OF *SIMON SAYS* FOR GOOD. HM? *HM?*

...a sabotaged pleasure cruiser...

...an unexpected (except to Simon Says) earthquake...

...an attempted kidnapping, and more.

On through the day, until...

OKAY, SIMON, IT'S *SIX O'CLOCK.*

YOU'VE *PROVED* YOUR POINT -- AND YOU'LL GET YOUR WISH. SEND ME THE *COORDINATES,* AND WE'LL BE THERE IN AN HOUR.

Starbright had talked to us the night before, sworn us to secrecy.

Maura, Ham, Ducky, Pete, a few others. No jocks, no cheerleaders. Mostly the weird kids, the outsiders.

The ones who'd actually liked Simon — or at least hadn't made fun of him — back when he was one of us.

It was kind of a scary idea, but Starbright picked the right kids. We were all intrigued, all curious about what it'd be like.

And he'd be on guard, which meant a lot.

OKAY, I'M *OUT* OF HERE. BUT I'LL BE NEARBY, LISTENING. ANY PROBLEMS, JUST *SHOUT.*

WE *KNOW.* IT'S TOO BAD YOU CAN'T COME TOO.

WASN'T THE *DEAL.*

But in the end, we couldn't say no. After all, who'd turn down a chance to attend...

...the 16th birthday party of Simon Says?!

You've got to figure. Everyone gets lonely. And being alone on your birthday sucks. Even for a teen genius mad scientist, right?

Simon wanted to be with kids his own age, for once. To have a party, instead of sitting in an empty lab.

Not something Starbright could say no to. Not after the rest of the day.

So there we were...

...and there he was.

HAPPY BIRTHDAY

It was weird, at first — he was a criminal mastermind, after all. And everyone was cautious.

But in the end, a party's a party...

...and it didn't take long before that's all it was.

A strange party, sure. But a party.

Simon was quieter than the rest of us. But Simon had always been quiet.

And we'd been his friends, before. Starbright had been good about that.

He'd rounded up the right people.

ICE CREAM, MAURA?

OH, *NO*, I COULDN'T -- WELL, MAYBE JUST A *LITTLE*...

ICE CREAM FOR THE *LADY*, SCOOP-1!

MEPS!

ICE CRE

And he looked... well, "happy" wasn't the right word. But after what we'd seen of him the past few years?

"Happier" certainly fit.

Even so, there was still something...

SIMON. HAPPY **BIRTHDAY.**

RICK! YOU DIDN'T **NEED** TO -- I SPECIFICALLY **TOLD** STARBRIGHT, NO PRESENTS!

YEAH, HE **SAID.**

BUT I FIGURED YOU WENT TO A LOT OF **TROUBLE** FOR THIS PARTY, SO...

A **BOOK?**

YOU'VE GOT ALL THE **SCIENCE** STUFF YOU COULD WANT, RIGHT? AND YOU'VE GOT TO PASS THE TIME. NO SCIENCE IN THAT. OR **COPS.** OR CRIME.

The Seventh Sword

HA! VERY THOUGHTFUL. THANK YOU.

YOU KNOW, YOU'RE STILL A **MINOR.** YOU COULD MAKE SOME SORT OF DEAL. WITH **YOUR** BRAIN, WITH ALL YOU CAN OFFER? YOU DON'T HAVE TO --

STOP.

I **LIKE** YOU, RICK. YOU'RE SMART, AND YOU **CARE** ABOUT THINGS.

BUT BE **HONEST.** THAT CHAIR -- WHEN YOU'RE IN IT, THAT'S ALL PEOPLE **SEE,** RIGHT? WHEN THEY SEE **ME,** IT'S... IT'S SIMILAR.

THEY DON'T **UNDERSTAND.** THEY NEVER WILL. **YOU** SEE DIFFERENT, I SEE DIFFERENT, BUT THEM? ALL **THEY** SEE --

ALL THEY **SEE...**

I got the impression he was talking about something that mattered deeply to him. But whatever it was, it wasn't the wanted-criminal thing...

152

THE *WHOLE BUILDING!* IT'S :UHH!: A GIANT --

CENTRIFUGE, YES.

ONE THAT CAN GENERATE *ENOUGH FORCE* TO CRUSH EVEN *YOU!*

THE FORCE ISN'T AS STRONG AT THE *CENTER.* IF I GOT THERE BEFORE IT HIT *FULL SPEED,* I COULD BREAK OUT.

I-IT'S *STRONG,* BUT --

IF -- IF I CAN --

TOOM

YOU *KNEW* THAT, OF COURSE. YOU COULD HAVE DONE *WORSE,* BUT THAT WAS AS CLOSE AS YOU CAN COME TO SAYING *THANK YOU.*

YOU'RE *WELCOME,* SIMON.

AND YOU DON'T HAVE TO DO *ANY* OF THIS. JUST BECAUSE PEOPLE *LOOK AT YOU,* AND SEE SOMETHING THEY DON'T *UNDERSTAND* --

-- IT DOESN'T MEAN *YOU* HAVE TO BE WHATEVER THEY *SEE.* IT'S UP TO *YOU.* ALL YOU HAVE TO DO --

I'd borrowed my dad's car as soon as I got home, and high-tailed it off to see if I could find the place.

I couldn't hear what Starbright said, though. Not until the end...

HAPPY BIRTHDAY, *SIMON SIEZMANSKI!* AND *MANY MORE!*

AND *THAT...*

THAT WAS THE LAST I EVER *SAW* OF HIM.

ALMOST THE LAST *ANYONE* SAW OF HIM.

I'M *BACK.*

HEY, S.

WHAT IS IT TONIGHT? STILL *SALLY?*

SARAH. I'M TRYING IT *OUT,* BUT I DON'T KNOW YET.

STILL DON'T WANT TO TRY *"SIMONE"?*

NO. TOO *CLOSE.*

HE'D BE *PROUD,* YOU KNOW. OF *ALL* OF THIS.

PROUD?

THIS *CAN'T* BE WHAT HE EXPECTED...

I DON'T *KNOW...*

IT WAS ONLY A *MONTH* LATER HE DIED.

AND IT WAS SO *LIKE* HIM.

HE'D PULLED SOME *GUNRUNNERS* OFF A BOAT IN THE SOUND. GOTTEN THEM TO *SAFETY*. GUNRUNNERS.

HE WOULDN'T RISK ANYONE ELSE'S LIFE, EVEN *THEIRS*. BUT HE KNEW THEY'D BEEN SMUGGLING *SOMETHING ELSE*, FOR A LOCAL *PYRAMID* CELL.

...AND *WHATEVER* IT WAS, IT WAS *ENOUGH*. EVEN WITH *HIS* POWER.

HE MUST'VE TRIED TO *DEACTIVATE* IT...

THEY RECOVERED THE BODY. IT WAS *CHET MARKHAM*. MARKHAM HIGH'S *STAR QUARTERBACK*. SCION OF THE *RICHEST FAMILY* IN TOWN.

IT WAS *CHET MARKHAM*. AND I -- I --

A-AUHH!

S-SIMON? WH -- ?

I TH-THOUGHT HE WAS *YOU!*

ME?

I THOUGHT -- *ENERGY TRANSFORMATION,* CHAIR MORPHED INTO THE ARMORED SUIT -- STUPID, SO *STUPID* --

BY RIGHTS, CHET MARKHAM SHOULD HAVE BEEN JUST ANOTHER *JERK,* LIKE THE OTHERS.

BUT HE *WASN'T.* HE'D BEEN A GOOD, KIND, *HOPEFUL* KID WHO WENT OUT OF HIS WAY TO --

IT'S, UH -- IT'S OKAY --

I C-CAN'T -- DIDN'T --

I WROTE THEM ALL *OFF.* WROTE THE *WORLD* OFF. ALL I FELT FROM THEM -- FOR THEM -- ALL I *LET* MYSELF FEEL WAS HATE AND ANGER --

H-HE WASN'T *FAKING* IT. HE W-WAS FOR REAL.

YES. HE *WAS.*

I THOUGHT STARBRIGHT HAD TO BE AN *OUTSIDER.* ANOTHER FREAK, WHO COULD *SYMPATHIZE* WITH THE FREAKS.

BUT IT WASN'T LIKE THAT. A *STRAIGHT WHITE BOY* WHO SAW HOPE FOR *EVERYONE* GOT ME TO SEE -- THAT MAYBE THERE *WAS* HOPE AFTER ALL.

A-AND THE *LAST THING* HE SAID TO ME...

FOR EVERYONE. EVEN FOR *ME.*

SO. YOU TOOK DOWN *MISTER TOAD.* HOW DO YOU *FEEL* ABOUT IT?

I... CAN *DO* THIS. NOT JAIL. I'M NOT TURNING MYSELF *IN.* BUT IF I CAN MAKE UP FOR THE WORST I DID, PAY THINGS *FORWARD...*

HERE IN *CONNECTICUT?*

NO. TOO CLOSE TO *HOME,* BOTH FOR SECURITY AND FOR IT TO FEEL LIKE A *FRESH START.* I'VE GOT *GLOBAL REACH,* WITH THESE POWERS...

...SO I WAS THINKING, I MIGHT BASE MYSELF IN *ASTRO CITY.* THEY'RE *USED* TO SUPERHEROES THERE. THEY'RE USED TO A *LOT* OF UNUSUAL THINGS.

BUT, UH... WOULD YOU *COME,* IF I DID?

I'M A *NOVELIST.* I CAN WORK FROM ANYWHERE. I'D BE *GLAD* TO.

AND -- HAVE YOU THOUGHT ABOUT A *NAME?*

I KEEP TELLING YOU, I'LL *FIND* THE RIGHT ONE.

BUT IT'S *NOT* GOING TO BE SIMONE. THAT'S JUST --

-- IT'S LIKE SAYING THE *REAL ME* IS JUST THE *OLD ME* WITH A COSMETIC CHANGE. THAT'S *NOT* --

WHOA, WHOA. THAT'S NOT WHAT I *MEANT.*

18 — returns
— face
— smile. Sally? Sarah.
    Not Simon L?
    No. Too close. Makes me feel fake.
        be proud   pected

19 — two months
    saving drug
    boom --
    from water

0 — weeping. W
    thought he u
    me?
    he was golden   veloped.
        He was y
    he mean'   no regret--

1 —   be h
                time t
            oset ing.
        no more tra
        no surgery   or   in his powers-- transfor
        ever fixed   k's spin

2   how do you feel?
        I can do this. Turn self in, no. But make up -- pay forward--
    where? Connecticut?
    Astro City

    PYRAMID cell

    Chet Markham. Quarterbac
        family in town. R, righ

            was one of them.
                But he never -- he

    Thought i   was against me
        But -- it   ike him cou

    I --
        don't know. Think o-
    He'd be   some one carrying it on--
    He always thought.
        I hope -- don't believe i -- destiny
    destiny-- exists, something worth
        Oh, yes ---

24 Broken Man ... you ll play a role. Very important role

silver adept

Since magicians are usually such a dour, serious lot, we wanted to play against type and make the Silver Adept look like a sexy party-girl of a magician. It fit her personality, and it's not our usual costume approach in ASTRO CITY.

We started with some awful sketches by me (below) and then Brent made it all actually look good.

The Silver Adept

open collar
+ tunic
held by
diamond
shape
navel
ring

no cleavage.
to collar

one piece
Add ring to navel

Yes, she even has a mystic tramp stamp. It has powers, too. Maybe someday we'll get to show you what they are...

We also had to make the Adept's house look (a) mystic and (b) lived-in. Brent did a stunning job.

When you need reference on bookshelves and clutter, look no further than an artist's studio!

Raitha McCann started out younger and slimmer. But not everyone in a superhero comic should be in perfect shape. So she changed.

"THE
NIGHTFLYING
LORD"
ACv3 #5
10-19-11

"THE
NIGHTFLYING
LORD"
ACv3 #5
10-19-11
rev. 9-6-12

A couple of versions of the Night-Flying Lord, changing him to a more impressive build and to oddly-carved stone armor.

stone sea mages

The Queen of Dust and Decay and Tumorr, on the other hand, looked great right from the start.

"TUMORR"
ACv3 #5
10-19-11

"STRAY"
AC #24
11-9-10

"STRAY"
AC #24
11-9-10
POWERED
MODE
REV. 2-14-11

"STRAY"
AC #24
11-9-10

stray

Stray was originally created for an Astro City movie treatment i wrote (which didn't end up going anywhere), but I liked her enough that when we started work on "The Deep Dark Woods," I asked Brent to design her up for Graham Nolan, and we added her in.

(And yes, there was already an Astro City hero named Stray, but times change, and names get reused...)

gundog

— OPEN HAIR STYLE

FULL SKULL CAP COVER OF LEATHER WITH STRAPS HANGING

CAN WE MIX BROWN LEATHER WITH BLACK SO HE HAS SOME BIT OF COLOR?

HE'S LIKE A GUN-TOTING HAWKEYE.

REDDISH BROWN MORE

Gundog was fun. We needed someone who'd get across a very strong impression right away, since we didn't have much room, so he needed to be simple, human and engaging. Alex's design for him sure was.

Gundog's car. Everything about him needs to say "hi-tech good ol' boy." I want to see this car again. Maybe in a chase scene.

Alex gave Gundog such a roguish bad-boy grin, Brent had to make sure he could duplicate it.

Laura had very little space to make an impression, too, and since we see her practically instantly (if temporarily) turn to crime — but we wanted readers to like her — she had to do it adorably. Brent took care of that.

When we started with the Dancing Master, we wanted something that felt old, formal, 19th-century at the latest. We tried that...

...but Alex found himself simplifying and updating his look...

MUCHA?

But we liked the older designs so much that I rewrote the script to establish that the D.M. enters this world in a very formal, courtly look, and the world affects him, so he changes over time, going from a Gustave Doré look...

...until we eventually settled on this Peter-Max-inspired design.

DANCING MASTER

dancing master

...to others, including Beardsley, Leyendecker and Mucha, and eventually to Peter Max and beyond.

robots

The first take on the Ballbearians was too much ball-bearing, not enough barbarian. The second struck the right balance.

I didn't want the Scandroid to have arms...but I did want him to be rideable. Brent fixed that with prehensile feet and a removable chairback.

Designing Mechismo was fun. I don't think I'd ever said of a robot design, "You know what he needs? He needs a big ol' handlebar mustache and chest hair."

And he did!

Alex's design and pencils for the cover to #14. We had a lot of robots in the story, but to make a powerful, iconic cover, it was best to focus on just one...

When I described the story of #14-15 to Alex, he said, "I've got the perfect cover model." And he did: A helpful relative of his named Dottie Thomas.

Oddly, she came out looking so much like my late mother-in-law, Phyllis Huntington, that we wound up sending Brent pictures of Phyllis at around college age to use in the flashback...

starbright

Young, heroic, positive, bold, iconic. But distinctive. Easy to say. Not always so easy to do, considering how many other heroes have fit that bill over the years...

SMOKE TRAIL?
BLUISH LIGHT TRAIL LIKE A COMET

WHITE WITH SILVER

GUN-METAL GRAY

Alex put Starbright in a containment suit, because he's got an energy-form, so the suit could keep him solid. The basic design of the suit came quickly, but the details were harder.

We kept saying, "Too dark" or "Too Legion-y" or occasionally, "Too Firestorm."

What his energy-self would look like was another concern.

RED STYLE BODYSUIT

"BLUE 'SPACY' HEAD"

NOT CHROME BUT SHINY VINYL LIKE ULTRAMAN COSTUMES

BLUE-WHITE HEAD GLOW

RED-WHITE HEAD GLOW

ENERGY TRAIL OF W W/ RED OUTLINE

MAIN SUIT WHITE WITH BLUE TRIM MAY SHINY WHITE VINYL?

WHITE WITH DARK METAL

RED-WHITE TAIL

Another possible spin on him...

...and Brent's adaptation of Starbright's male costume to a female form, for the third-act reveal. He changed her emblem a bit, but in the actual story we changed it even further, just to differentiate them more.

ASTRO CITY 16

astro city 16

Alex's first design for the cover to #16, and his final design. We worked out the "plot" of this page (such as it is) over the phone, and then I wrote a script for him to draw from. Or maybe I wrote it after his final layout. Either way, it worked!

— KURT BUSIEK

about the creators

KURT BUSIEK broke into comics after graduating college in 1982. Since then, he's been an editor, a literary agent, a sales manager and more, but is best known as the multiple-award-winning writer of *Astro City, Marvels, Superman, Conan, Arrowsmith, Superstar, Shockrockets* and many others. He lives in the Pacific Northwest.

BRENT ANDERSON began making his own comics in junior high school, and graduated to professional work less than a decade later. He's drawn such projects as *Ka-Zar the Savage, X-Men: God Loves Man Kills, Strikeforce: Morituri, Somerset Holmes, Rising Stars* and, of course, *Astro City,* for which he's won multiple Eisner and Harvey Awards. He makes his home in Northern California.

GRAHAM NOLAN has been writing and illustrating comics since 1984. He's worked on an array of characters from Superman to the X-Men, and was senior illustrator on *Detective Comics* for 6 years. An award winning artist, Nolan is also the co-creator of the iconic Batman villain Bane.

ALEX ROSS worked on *Terminator: The Burning Earth* and *Clive Barker's Hellraiser* before *Marvels* made him an overnight superstar. Since then, he's painted, plotted and/or written such series as *Kingdom Come, Superman: Peace on Earth, Justice, Earth X* and *Project Superpowers,* and won over two dozen industry awards.

ALEX SINCLAIR has colored virtually every character DC Comics has, and more besides. Best known for his work with Jim Lee and Scott Williams, he's worked on such books as *Batman: Hush, Superman: For Tomorrow, Blackest Night, Batman & Robin, Wonder Woman, Arrowsmith* and *Kingdom Come: Superman.*

WENDY BROOME was a longtime member of the coloring staff at Wildstorm Studios before going freelance in 2004. She's made a specialty of large-cast books, including *Wildcats 3.0, The Authority, Gen13, The End League, Thundercats* and *Top 10* as well as pitching in as needed on *Astro City.*

JOHN ROSHELL joined Comicraft in 1992, helping propel the lettering/design studio to its position in the industry. He's lettered thousands of comics pages, along with creating logos and fonts, designing book editions and more. He also writes the series *Charley Loves Robots,* which appears in *Elephantmen.*